Out of Love in Spring

poems by

Hailey Spencer

Finishing Line Press
Georgetown, Kentucky

Out of Love in Spring

Copyright © 2022 by Hailey Spencer
ISBN 978-1-64662-989-3 First Edition
All rights reserved under International and Pan-American Copyright Conventions. No part of this book may be reproduced in any manner whatsoever without written permission from the publisher, except in the case of brief quotations embodied in critical articles and reviews.

ACKNOWLEDGMENTS

Several of these poems have been previously published:

"Lycanthrope" in *Coffin Bell Journal*
"Towns that Trigger" in *Hairstreak Butterfly Review*
"A Spell for Drowning Ghosts" in *Levitate*
"Three Blows from a Hatchet" in *The Festival Review*
"Monstrous Woman" and "Beneath the Scales" in the *Primeval Monster* Zine
"What to Write in Your Journal to Move On" in *Atlas and Alice*
"Application 17: Hardware Store" in *Peatsmoke Journal*
"Theories About the Universe" in *Project Green Gables*
"Date Night in the Time of Global Pandemic" in *Press Pause Press*
"August" in *You Might Need to Hear This*

Publisher: Leah Huete de Maines
Editor: Christen Kincaid
Cover Art: Amy Deyerle-Smith
Author Photo: Elizabeth Nellams
Cover Design: Elizabeth Maines McCleavy

Order online: www.finishinglinepress.com
also available on amazon.com

Author inquiries and mail orders:
Finishing Line Press
PO Box 1626
Georgetown, Kentucky 40324
USA

Table of Contents

Part One

boy on the bus whose gauges make me want to jump off a bridge 1

Slow Rolling Boil 2

Lycanthrope... 3

(self) destruction 4

Part Two

Towns that Trigger 7

A Spell for Drowning Ghosts... 8

Three Blows from a Hatchet.. 9

Monstrous Woman... 10

Part Three

Fourth Date 13

Beneath the Scales 14

What to Write in Your Journal to Move On.................................. 16

application #17: hardware store.. 18

Part Four

Theories about the Universe 23

Date Night in the Time of Global Pandemic 25

August 26

In a Time of Pandemic 27

Part One

I never thought I'd
self-destruct from just the sound
of my own heartbeat.

**boy on the bus whose gauges make me want
to jump off a bridge**

greasy undercut and ink-stained skin
the layers of his button-down ride up
revealing the angles of his naked wrists
every unveiling leaves me aching
those veins across his hands
round burns from cigarette flame make up
the million eyes of an angel,
be not afraid
I want to maim him
tear his flesh so his blood's in my veins
he makes me want to destroy myself
and chain my new body to his image
I can see the world through the tunnels in his earlobes
stage my escape by mapping his tattoos

I think he might be the patron saint of pain.
I've been waiting at his altar all my life.

Slow Rolling Boil

Temptation in a teapot,
the soft sad that seeps under your skin.
I want him / like I want to stay in bed.

His ignorance is bliss.
He doesn't know about the snakes
between my sheets / whispering.

He hasn't heard the lies they like to tell.
The simple truth of sex
is: sweat slipping

between bodies, something essential
and easy to ignore. He doesn't know.
What happens next:

the universe is full of particles,
the steeping of a thousand tiny leaves.
Slowly, I am submerged.

Lycanthrope

Your body is a loose uncanny thing, teeth
not mossy boulders, but not tiny pearls either
and I'm sorry we took the time to know each other.
I'm sorry that I looked at your hands

and all I saw were claws, your teeth only fangs,
I'm sorry that you only have two hands
and one of them is always busy with something else.
I'm sorry my angles aren't sharp enough yet.

My body is trapped in a bog, suffocated in peat
and other objects I can't really name. I'm lying;
I don't know what peat is and I might be afraid of it.
My body is the place where a bridge is not.

(self) destruction

You never saw me coming.
Knuckles bruised from pounding against
my shattered expectations of who I would be by now.
I want you like I want to get into a fight.

Knuckles bruised from pounding against
the contours of your body, pain I never knew I needed.
I want you like I want to get into a fight—
but I never learned to throw a punch.

The contours of your body, pain I never knew. I needed
to feel my pulse throbbing in your ears.
But I never learned to throw a punch,
and I hate the sight of blood,

too. Feel my pulse throbbing in your ears,
against your ribcage, searching for something that isn't there
(and I hate the sight of blood
but it's a sacrifice I'm willing to make).

Against your ribcage, searching for something that isn't there,
like a moth, beating myself against a lightbulb.
But it's a sacrifice I'm willing to make.
(I never learned to fight fair.)

Like a moth, beating myself against a lightbulb:
My shattered expectations of who I would be by now.
I never learned to fight fair.
You never saw me coming.

Part Two

You destroy yourself
so fucking beautifully.

Towns That Trigger

There are places where it's not safe to walk
    After dark
    When you've had too much
        or not enough
        to drink
    In the fluorescent landscape of your dreams
    (Ever, in any state of being)
The memory of escape is hazy,

(breaking down bones so you could slide out through the cracks)

leaving behind a year's worth of reminders, including
    Apologies written on crumpled napkins
    Stories that contain the words
        safe, home, we,
        or fruit fly
    One pillow, one blanket, two sheets
    A mind filled with something

        other than broken glass.

A Spell for Drowning Ghosts

1. Slip the dagger from your hand and rest it against your diminished hip bones. Your body maps an undiscovered landscape, vast and full of dragons. Ragged nails dig in against the skin.

2. Fill up the bathtub and wash your sheets, dipping them until the invisible lover unfurls her fingers and lets go. Invest in a new pillow. In the afternoons, sleep will dance across your heavy lids. It will not last until evening.

3. Place a candle in the lopsided clay mug you made in sixth grade. Strike a match, and allow it to burn out. Strike a second match and blow it out yourself.

4. Ramble through the hills of your ill-favored images, until the ambiguity of the past no longer intimidates you. Step into the shadows trusting that there is an exit. You are the background noise of wistful bliss. You are your own compass and lantern-holder.

5. In the landscape of your being is a gash. Sketch its outline into the sand, tracing the sound of its echo bouncing back.

6. List your fears, first silent, then aloud.

Three Blows from a Hatchet

For two weeks straight I prayed that I'd stay sad,
last summer. Knee deep in hailstorms and
the feelings that ate their way out of me
the way worms creep in and out of cadavers.

Last summer, need deep in hailstorms, and
the house we were making. The weeds we had to dig out of
the way. Worms crept in. And out of the cadaver
of the blue-jay we buried in secret, grapevines grew.

The house we were making. The weeds. We had to crawl out of
the traps we'd found our ways into. Sometimes I dream
of the blue-jay. We buried secrets, grew grapes.
Beneath the dirt its neck was snapped and we didn't tell a soul

about the traps we'd found our ways into. Sometimes I dream
of the feelings that ate their way out of me.
Beneath the dirt the bird's neck was snapped. We didn't tell a soul
for two weeks straight. We prayed. We stayed sad.

Monstrous Woman

I live a life of quiet lycanthropy.
Silver teeth with bloodstains underneath;
translucent skin across my sides and front.
My voice a piercing echo of my mother's.

I live in a toolshed with un-white rugs.
Locusts in my bathtub, hydrangea on the windowsill.
Wallpaper peeling to show fungus underneath.
In the pale light of morning I lay out crisp new sheets.

I sit and watch the wings circle the drain.
My eyes are glassy. I grind my teeth at night.
My skin is red with cobwebs where I've grown.
I scribble on my walls and it is art.

I haven't slept in weeks. My fingers dance
across the gossamers. I itch to tear apart
my own ribcage with my own fingernails, sharp
with just a little dirt under the edges.

Part Three

You should really know:
it's not love pulling me to
you, just gravity.

Fourth Date

We fucked inside your tiny room
and scavenged from the fridge.
Hands clasped, we walked along a trail.
We kissed on every bridge.

Your lips were soft and sweet as they
laid kisses down my spine.
We stumbled down the narrow path.
The sunset smelled like pine.

And every time we kissed I was
the first to pull away.
My lips were sticky with the words
I knew I wouldn't say.

I almost knew I loved you then
in summer's warm embrace.
I pushed away the thought, but still
trailed fingers down your face.

The bridges did not let me fall
but held me without fail.
It became easier to cross.
I let go of the rail.

After a while the sun went down.
The creek was almost dry.
You drove me home. The stars were out.
Your hand was on my thigh.

Beneath the Scales

I. Last night I dreamed that we unzipped our
skin, and to our surprise we found that
underneath everything
we weren't monsters after all.

II. Lately I've been scratching myself raw,
all tooth and claw and maybe if I took myself apart
I could put myself back together in a way that wasn't so
destructive.

III. I stopped being lonely when I met you.

IV. I always knew deep down that you weren't a monster. You
were just the one who taught me how to embrace people
without flinching. You reached inside my skin and unzipped
my armored scales, left me vulnerable.

But you weren't a monster, not ever.

V. Underneath my skin is the girl that loves you.
I want her to disappear. I want her to dissolve
into gold, reemerge as something stronger.
Steel.
Titanium.
Scales, teeth, and claws.

VI. I didn't know what it meant to be lonely until I met you.

VII. In my dream, we unzipped our skin
let the titanium plating fall to the ground
& looked each other in the eye.

VIII. I was supposed to be a monster,
armored skin protecting me from
the hero's sword.
No one was supposed to get close
enough to look beneath the scales.

IX. I didn't know what it meant to be human until I met you.

X. Last night, we unzipped our skin.
I thought it'd be a relief to be human for a change.
But to my surprise, I found
that I missed the smell of smoke
from the villages I left burning in my wake.

What To Write in Your Journal To Move On

1. *A description of what happened.*

To transmogrify biography to story, certain details must be omitted for the sake of time. Do I drown out my lover's unbrushed hair, the day I picked blackberries when all he wanted to do was kiss? The intimacy of an almost-remembered coffee order? What do I disclose and what do I obscure? Is description definition?

2. *How it left you feeling.*

The last time we kissed was in the hallway before I took a sledgehammer to the walls. Half of my bedroom was paneled in mirrors and I watched his long thick hair as I prayed to the goddess of lies.

3. *Who was there and what they said and did.*

He said, "I'm moving to New York."
He said, "There's nothing for me here."
He said, "I'm sorry, I'm so fucking sorry."

I said, "I love you."
I said, "I love you."
I said, "I'll go."

He went.
I didn't.

4. *What you wish had happened instead.*

We live together in a tiny apartment above a pizza shop, and we fight and we fuck and make art and sleeping in his arms has never felt better and I am deliriously happy.

We live together in a tiny apartment that is too hot in summer and too cold in winter, and we fight and we fight and the art I make is small and I can't sleep with his arms this tight around me.

5. *Steps you could take to start moving on.*

[answer left blank due to time]

application #17: hardware store

1.   What do you want to accomplish in the next 12 months?

o   Twelve months, a single slippery year during which I will sit in a tub immersed by sprigs of rosemary. I will strike a match for each day I survive, try to forgive the image in my mirror.

o   Last January I had a lover who let bananas go black in his car. His plan: to be an actor in Manhattan, and I would be the understanding girl with the messy topknot and the fox tattoo that tagged along.

o   I just need a way to pay my bills.

o   Other (please specify) _____
_____

2.   Where do you see yourself five years from now?

o   Somewhere across the sea sit castles without caretakers. To stay intact they need a savior, someone to play solitaire with the ghosts and salt down the fungus as it skims across dead stone.

o   I tell myself I will be a writer. In the mornings I will put pencil to paper, and I won't look up until lunch. I will write every day, even the hard days, even the hard years.

o   My yard is a garden of weeds, bumblebees dancing in a pre-shrunk dream of clover and dandelion. I make plans to dig them out, but never do.

o   Other (please specify) _____
_____

3.   What ambitions or goals would you like to pursue at this job?

o   At 4am, I find myself in the kitchen, my new love still awake and draining pasta. The dark outside is the dark in an old favorite book, but this is not what romance looks like, only tired. I love her best the month I finally sleep.

o   I pictured it for so long: fox tattoo, topknot that's an artist's kind of sloppy, walking through the Trader Joes with empty pockets but always enough money to buy the nice olive oil.

o   I've been told I work well with people. Maybe I can do something with that.

o   Other (please specify) _____
_____

4. *How long do you see yourself working here?*

o   A week.

o   A lifetime.

o   Just until this whole writing thing takes off.

o   Other (please specify) _____
_____

5. *Briefly describe any physical or mental health issues we need to know about that could interfere with your ability to work in this environment, or prevent you from being a reliable employee.*

o   Last winter I said no to the rotten banana peels, no to Manhattan and yes to a job in Seattle I didn't want anymore. I ignored my hair and bought the one-month bus pass, and I scribbled endlessly but wrote nothing.

o   Dysthymia (n.) A mood disorder characterized by chronic mildly depressed or irritable mood often accompanied by other symptoms (such as eating and sleeping disturbances, fatigue, and poor self-esteem). —**From the Meriam-Webster dictionary, accessed online.**

o   I wish for lingering summer nights when the moon reaches down to kiss me on the cheek. I wish for simple meaning. I wish for geese, flying through the sky with scarves beneath their chins, tying them down for the winter.

o   Other (please specify) _____
_____

Part Four

There's always
something

underneath.

Go look.

Theories about the Universe

Gravity
the force that attracts a body toward the center of the earth,
or toward any other physical body having mass

Having a dream about someone you barely know. Being taken by surprise. People who lean in to listen. The first time you notice the color of her eyes. When a song suddenly applies to your life in a way you'd never have expected. The giddy feeling of having a secret. The person you see on the bus every day but never speak to.

Inertia
a property of matter by which it continues in its existing state,
unless that state is changed by an external force

Kissing in the hail. Strong arms holding you even when you feel like you're too much or not enough. The jittery feeling in your stomach before a first date. Eye-contact with a beautiful stranger. Seeing a familiar person in an unfamiliar place. A good-night text. Unexpected memories hidden in desk drawers.

Entropy
lack of order or predictability;
gradual decline into disorder

Checking your phone every five minutes for a text that never comes. Memories of a life that doesn't quite feel like your own. The moment when you look in a mirror and can't recognize your own face. The words, "I love you, but not like that." Researching the definition of the word "goodbye." Writing a poem about it. Unwriting a poem about it. Having a dream about someone you don't know anymore.

Probability
the extent to which an event is likely to occur

Falling out of love in spring.

Date Night in the Time of Global Pandemic

Standing in line at the drive-in,
Elizabeth inches forward, waiting
for her burger. I clutch my greasy bag:
fries and a chocolate shake.
The mask my mother stitched me
clings to the margins of my ears.

Through my glasses' built-up steam
is a man. White hair, mostly bald
fiddling with his paper respirator,
the type Elizabeth and I might have worn
last April, digging the backyard
to lay out lines of bricks.

(We built a firepit together;
recycled brick, a tiny hill of sand
and our bare fingers, sinking in the dirt.
I ripped out the landscaping fabric.
She lifted up and let spill the bags of sand.
I laid the bricks.)

This April, the man stands
on a chalk-drawn line, six feet away.
His eyes smile.
He tells us that this is the first time
he's gone outside in nine weeks.
He orders five large burgers and six fries.

Elizabeth's food is slid through a plastic window.
The sky begins a careful *drip drip drip*.
Our sandals slip. We climb the little hill
outside the library's zip-tied doors,
slide our masks into a canvas bag
and eat our fries under a drizzling sky.

August

Sweat slips down my spine
listless summertime heat and
the things I didn't expect
to be feeling so soon after the last time.
This isn't how I thought things would go but I am learning that
summers, like second chances, only come around once.
Sweat slips down my spine
it's too hot to sleep and I
keep having those conversations that can only happen in the dark,
keep sending myself back down the
cobwebbed corridors of the past
toward things that are not sad but dry,
like how the skies have been dry, and
there's so many things I want to say to you, like
it broke 90 degrees again today, and
summers are like second chances no two are the same, and
do you believe in ghosts because I swear I've been seeing them.
I've always thought that summer was for ghosts, or at least for
the empty feeling of cotton candy placed on your tongue by the boy
who loved you at fifteen but by sixteen had forgotten your name.
And I wish I could drown the specters, but
we've been in a drought since March so there's nothing to do but
watch them multiply, like mosquitos,
like suppressed emotions that you can't
hold back any longer.
Sweat slips down my spine.
I spend a lot of time wondering
when it will rain, why I keep
getting second chances, whether
or not the heat
will break.

In a Time of Pandemic
in the mode of Ilya Kaminsky

Pedaling my way up North Seattle's deep ridges,
I watch my neighbors

don fabric masks to sit in their back yards.
The woman next door, from six feet away,
asks me to check my compost bin
she's found dead rats near hers.

It is a summer of quiet.

I slip on the mask my mother sewed me—
yellow trees, my favorite color—
and walk to the convenience store
to pick up cake mix
and red wine.

In this city, test results take
72 hours and a painful swab up the nostril
after which I sit in the yard.

The neighbor was telling the truth.
There is a rat, partially decomposed
I lift it with the shovel—

one bag, tied, another, tied again
taken out on garbage day.

It is a quiet summer.

I hear the kids racing up and down the street
with no clear start date for school
as lines of worry form
between their parents' eyebrows

and I,
childless and unemployed, I

sit on my patio with a new book
and smile (forgive me)
smile as I crack the spine.

Hailey Spencer is, in the words of her wife Elizabeth, an absolute cloud of a girl. She is obsessed with fairy tales and has an equally passionate rivalry with ants. She lives and writes in Seattle. For more on Hailey and her work, visit haileyspencerwrites.com

www.ingramcontent.com/pod-product-compliance
Lightning Source LLC
LaVergne TN
LVHW041513070426
835507LV00012B/1529